How To Save Money On Your Wedding Day

Finally Revealed: Simple and Easy to Follow Methods of Saving Thousands on your Big Day but still making it a Fantastic Day to Remember!

Author: C B Foster

"A successful marriage requires falling in love many times, always with the same person."

– Germaine Greer

Table of Content

CHAPTER ONE: You're engaged! Now What?

Wedding Savings Trend #1

CHAPTER TWO: The Crew, Dress & Tux

Wedding Savings Trend #2

CHAPTER THREE: The Reception

Wedding Savings Trend #3

CHAPTER FOUR: Video & Photography

CHAPTER ONE

You're Engaged! Now What?

Wedding Savings Trend#1
(Couples are choosing to get married on Thursday, Friday or Sunday nights. Those days are less expensive than Saturday weddings.)

Can you believe Weddings Savings Trend #1? Saturdays have been the wedding day of choice for years. But a new day is dawning. Folks have figured out that it's cheaper to get married on Thursdays, Fridays and Sunday nights. Sunday nights before a long holiday weekend is the most popular. The Fourth of July is also a big choice. Hmm, that's really something to think about, now isn't it?

THE PRE-PLANNING STAGE (LA-DE-DAH)

We started out with this wedding trend because I wanted you to start thinking about what day you want to get married on. It's cheaper to get married on any other day EXCEPT Saturday. You'll have to make the decision if any other day will work for you. I can understand if you're hell bent on getting married on a Saturday because it has been historically the most common wedding day.

We'll just figure out another way to save you money if you decide to get married on a Saturday. Don't fret!   We have a whole array of cost saving measures throughout this book. Don't try to decide on a day just yet. I just want to get you to thinking in the cost saving mode. We'll come back to planning the exact time, day and location of your wedding a little later in the book, but, for right now, let's talk about the pre-planning wedding stage or what I call the "la di dah stage."

If you haven't done so already, you'll want to spread the news to all of your loved ones. I understand that. In fact, you may want to tell everyone you come in contact with today that you're in love and you're getting married. Rest assured, this is all very normal. The pre-planning stage is the most important part of wedding planning.

You decide on a wedding budget during this stage of the planning process. You'll decide on what you can afford and what you can't. You'll decide on the things you must have versus the things you can live without. You may not be able to afford all the lavish things you want for your wedding, but I'll show you ways to make some things affordable.

That's it in a nutshell. The key to planning a wedding on a budget is deciding on what you want to spend a whole lot on. You have to decide what things you won't skimp on. I've found a lot of couples have one thing in common when it comes to wedding planning. They all want a memorable event. We'll look at ways you can do that as well.

Planning a wedding is a huge undertaking. I have determined that there are several areas that will need your concentration if you're going to SAVE BIG MONEY on your wedding costs. You'll need to have what I call a sit down heart to heart with your fiancé. This heart to heart will help you to determine what is a priority for you as a couple.

You'll need to determine if there are certain things specific to the wedding that you must have. It could be that you want a certain band to play or a certain color to wear. It could be a certain location for the wedding or reception. I know a bride who was hell bent on having her wedding at an exclusive resort. The wedding chapel was in the midst of a garden beyond belief. While they spent a ton on money reserving the location, they saved money because they didn't have to buy flowers. Once you determine your must haves, you can then begin to incorporate them into your wedding.

EIGHT AREAS YOU CAN SAVE THE MOST

I've determined that there are eight areas where you can save the most on wedding costs. Here they are.

1. Food
2. Bar
3. Wedding Attire
4. Flowers
5. Photography & Videography
6. Music
7. Honeymoon
8. Guest List

Look at these areas and start thinking in the cost saving mode. Food and bar costs are one of the biggest expenses you'll have. You may decide to have a buffet or cater the reception yourself. You may decide to have an open bar for an hour or not to serve alcohol at all. These are all cost saving measures that you will want to think about.

The location where you're going to have the reception is also a big expense. Parks, forest preserves and a home backyard are all viable options for you. You'll see that I added wedding attire to the list of the areas where you can save the most money. As we go through the wedding planning process, you'll want to keep an eye out for discounted wedding attire.

You can also find some great deals on flowers if you know how to look and what you're looking for. I've put together a list of more than 250 flowers and plants to help you decide. A wedding wouldn't be a wedding without the romantic mood that only flowers can provide.

I had to add the photographer and videographer to the list of biggest expenses. You will have to pay for a good one there's really no way around that! But, there are ways to skimp without missing out on the memories. You have to capture the moment of your wedding as only these two professionals can do.

Everyone who is anyone will want to attend your wedding! It's inevitable that someone is going to be disappointed because they were not invited. However, keeping a tight lid on your guest list is very important to living within a budget. A good rule of thumb is not to invite more guests then you can spend a minute with.

CAN YOU BE YOUR OWN WEDDING CONSULTANT?

I'm often asked, "Do I need a wedding consultant. My response is usually, I don't know, do you?" A wedding consultant is responsible for helping to plan the wedding from the beginning to the very end. Theoretically, you can do this yourself. Some people save money by having a wedding consultant only on the day of the wedding. I believe this is a good way to save money as well.

A lot of times a church, reception hall, hotel and other venues will provide you with a wedding consultant on the day of the wedding as part of your package. Some other wedding consultants charge as much as 15% of the total money spent on the wedding. It's a good idea to go with a wedding consultant who is affiliated with a professional wedding organization. I list some of these organizations at the back of the book.

You're in for the thrill of your life if you decide to coordinate your own wedding! I'm going to show you how to do it coming up next so get ready! One of the first things you'll want to do is sit down and plan out a budget for your wedding. I always suggest creating your dream wedding.

COORDINATING A WEDDING

Your plans should be the best-case scenario. You've heard the old saying what the mind can conceive and believe; it can achieve? Bet you didn't know the author of that was talking about wedding planning. Well, maybe he wasn't, but I can assure you, he could've been.

Get a pen and paper ready. I want you to sit back, relax and envision what the perfect U-wedding would look like. Go through every detail from the colors that your attendants are wearing to the time of day it is. Imagine what your dress will look like and where the reception will be. Imagine for about fifteen minutes, and then come back to me.

Now, you're ready to begin the exciting process of wedding planning. You'll need a three ring binder, loose-leaf writing paper and notebook dividers with tabs. You'll proceed to organize all of the information you'll gather in the coming weeks and months ahead in this notebook.

Here's the headings you'll need for every section in your notebook.

1 Calendar
2 Budget
3 Clothing
4 Ceremony
5 Flowers
6 Decorations
7 Reception
8 Food
9 Videography/Photography
10 Guest/gift list

I'll give you my Four Month Calendar Guide a little later in Chapter 7. I'll show you what to do when. If you follow my calendar guide, you'll end up right on schedule. Let's talk for a moment about the budget.

DEVELOPING A BUDGET

The budget is important for obvious reasons. You don't want to end up spending yourself into a divorce before you're even married do you? A budget gives you strict guidelines to follow. Overspending will not necessarily give you the wedding of your dreams. The idea is to do it well without emptying out your pockets.

This gives you and idea of what your budget should look like percentage wise. Take a look at it.

1	Reception	50%
2	Bride's Dress, Shoes, Garter	15%
3	Videographer/Photographer	10%
4	Music	10%
5	Flowers	10%
6	Decorations	2%
7	Invitations/thank you cards	2%
8	Postage	1%

100%

I know what you're thinking. So many decisions, so little time. You'll need some help along the way. Solicit any and everybody you care about to help you. There are several things you'll need to do right away. Here they are.

1 Meet with parents
2 Pick a date
3 Reserve the ceremony and reception locations
4 Pick your wedding party
5 Meet with minister or rabbi
6 Choose a color theme and scheme

7   Begin guest list
8   Select a wedding dress, mother's dresses and
    bridesmaid dresses

There are a lot of decisions to be made right. Aren't you glad that you're soliciting the help from the people close to you? One decision you'll also have to make is whether you'll need a wedding consultant. You can SAVE a few hundred dollars if you can work this out without a consultant. But, I'll tell you; I have seen very few people who can. However, it is not impossible.

THREE TRADITIONAL THEMES

A budget may be the first thing a wedding coordinator will want to go over with you. But, a wedding theme is the second. You don't have to have one, however a wedding theme can give you some direction with your planning. For instance, I recently attended a theme wedding where the couple played out Cinderella complete with glass slipper and horse drawn buggy. None of the bridesmaids could fit the glass slipper. It was really cute. Take a look at these themes and let me know what you think!

Rose Riches

As its name suggests, roses, roses and more roses make up the theme to this wedding. The idea is to buy as many as you can afford, then fill in the gaps with lots of greenery. I've known people to beg, borrow and steal from relatives to get the potted plants out of homes and backyards. You'll save a lot of money that way. You can also use ribbons in the color scheme that you're using to tie around the plants. You can even add silk plants in with the live ones to add a dramatic effect. You can add wrought iron benches to create the garden affect as well.

In The Park

This theme is as its name suggests. You can pick a park to get married in and ship in more and flowers as needed. I've known couples that added everything from candle towers to portable streetlights at night to create the desired affect.

Hearts Mixed With Flowers

You'll want to use lots of hearts all over the place with this theme. You can buy many different kinds of heart shaped items in your local party store. If you're really looking to save money, you can make your own. I know a couple that made hearts out of construction materials like poster boards. My favorite hearts shaped items are thrown on tables for decoration. The pink, red, gold and silver like hearts are about the size of a flat pea. You throw them on the table and they sparkle.

EIGHT NONTRADITIONAL THEMES

Non-traditional theme weddings often have one thing in common. Elaborate costuming and dramatic effects. Let's take a look at eight of the most common nontraditional weddings.

All Hallow' Eve

Halloween is a favorite event for a lot of people including kids. It's not odd that once you grow up that you'd want to get married on one of your most favorite occasions, right? Halloween weddings include costumes and a masquerade ball type of event. You can downplay the harsh orange and black colors of Halloween by mixing in other colors like grays, silvers and white. I've also seen people use pumpkins with smiley faces as table decorations. Orange and black candles also create a lively affect.

Balloons

Balloons can create the same dramatic affect that flowers cans. You can hang them in the doorway to the reception or wedding hall. You can tie them to chairs. You can even use the bouquets on the tables as centerpieces. You can take your pick, cover the ceiling with a helium blown balloon or cover the floor with a hot air blown balloon. The idea is to have balloons everywhere! This is a very cost effective theme.

Celtic

Celtic weddings are booming right now! They are similar to renaissance weddings in that you'll need an old castle or outdoor setting in order to pull it off. The bride wears an ivory satin gown and a flowered wreath. The groom wears plaid tartans, kilts and kneed high white socks.

Country 'N Western

Get your blue jeans and line dancing shoes ready. You're in for a foot stomping, hand clapping good time. The food for the day is barbeque and potato salad. The reception hall is lined with red and white-checkered tablecloths. You can pull this theme off on a real life ranch or outside in a big backyard. Let your imagination run wild as far as decorations are concerned. You can use anything from cowboy hats to red bandanas. Let's move from the old west to the south of the border.

Fiesta

Have fun planning a Mexican fiesta! This theme is for people who enjoy the culture and the people. You can enjoy authentic Mexican food including tacos and burritos. You can also have fun decorating using piñatas and paper crepe flowers. Perhaps the warmth of Mexico isn't your only option. Try a wedding them that takes you across the Pacific.

Polynesian

Okay, so you may not be able to duplicate the Pacific Ocean for a Polynesian wedding. Any body of water will do! All you need are authentic music, tiki torches, flower leis and crepe paper flowers to get you in the mood here. The food is relatively inexpensive including from roast pork to fresh fruit.

Renaissance

Renaissance weddings are similar to a Celtic wedding in that you'll need elaborate costuming. They also take place outside or on the grounds of an old castle. The bride wears a heavy gown similar to what they use to wear in the 14th century. It has bell shaped sleeves and a V back line. The groom and his groomsmen wear velvet doublets and shirts with billowing sleeves. A feathered hat and sword tops off the man of the hour's wardrobe.

The Ole South

This is another wedding theme that takes place mainly outdoors. You'll need a beautiful mansion or plantation to help pull this theme off. The bride wears a southern belle wedding dress complete with parasol. The bridesmaid's dresses are also ball gowns. The groom and his groomsmen wear white dinner jackets and black pants. I hope you have some idea of the kind of theme wedding you'd like to have now that we've run through the most popular ones.

10 ETHNIC RITUALS

Once you decide what theme you want, it will become easier to plan some events around that theme. Did you know that some themes reflect your ethnic heritage? Well it does. Let's take a quick look at how ethnicity is connected to us.

1. African American couples celebrate what's called a "jumping of the broom." This happens immediately after the "I do's.

2. Chinese couples drink wine from goblets that are tied together with a red ribbon.

3. East Indian grooms get a turmeric paste rubbed all over their face to keep the bad spirits away.

4. German brides carry salted bread in their pocket and the groom carries grain to bring wealth into the household

5. Egyptian brides get their right wrist tied to the grooms left wrist.

6. English brides get a live or imitation spider placed in their gown by their guests.

7. French couples drink wind from a two cup that has two handles.

8. Greek brides receive money pinned to their gowns while dancing with her new husband during the reception.

9. Italian grooms get their ties cut into small pieces. The pieces are sold to the guests.

10. Korean couples feed their guests noodle soup to symbolize a happy life together.

These are just some of the rituals that are performed based on ethnicity. Did you recognize any of them? Do you want to include any of them as part of your wedding celebration? You can really make your wedding unique by incorporating a ritual. Hmm, just something to think about.

CHAPTER TWO

The Crew, White Dress & Tux

Wedding Savings Trend #2
*(Couples are saving money by buying wedding cakes,
flowers and reception food from the local supermarkets.)*

Well, who would've thought our Wedding Saving
Trend #2? Our research shows that couples are flocking to
the local grocer for wedding finger food like chicken wings
and cheese crackers.   They are also saving money over
catered prices for salads, vegetable platters, etc. Cake is
the biggest buy. You can save at least 15% by buying your
wedding cake depending on the size from a supermarket.

We'll talk a little bit more about how to save on
wedding reception costs a little later. But, for right now,
let's talk about saving money on one of the most important
stars of your wedding. Did you really think it was going to
be you?

MEET THE KEY PLAYERS

Talk to any wedding consultant and they will tell you.
There are several key people that you'll need to pull your
wedding off.   Of course, your parents will be on hand to
help if they can. The minister and musicians is also
important people. However, I'd say your wedding party is
very, very important.

Next to you, they are the people everyone is going to be
gazing at. What do they have on? How is the hair and
makeup styled?   Shoes, do the shoes match perfectly?
These are all questions your guests are going to ask as they

watch your wedding party parade up and down the aisle. So of course, these are the key players aka stars.

1 Matron or Maid of Honor
2 Best Man
3 Groomsmen
4 Bridesmaids

Now, let's look at how they are supposed to assist you in the days leading up to D-Day.

The Matron or Maid of Honor is the bride's right hand woman the wedding day. She helps the bride get dressed. She distributes the corsages and boutonnieres. She fixes the bride's train during the ceremony. She is the official witness to the vows. But, her duties actually begin long before then. She helps to address invitations and thank you notes. She helps to

The Best Man is the groom's right hand guy. He is in charge of making sure everything and I mean everything runs smooth. He is the official witness to the vows, however he has many more duties. He pays the clergy He handles the groom's travel, supervises ushers, holds the rings and marriage license, and delivers the toast.

The Groomsmen on the other hand have many duties on the wedding day. They are usually the first people who guests see when they come to the wedding. It is there duty to meet and greet the guests. Seat them on the proper side of the church aisle if there is one. Groomsmen also seat the bride and grooms mothers. In some cases, groomsmen also arrange for the transportation of the bridesmaids. Now, if your wedding is so big that you're having groomsmen and ushers, then it is up to the ushers to seat the guests.

Bridesmaid's main duty is to look pretty and happy on the wedding day! No joke. If you're a bridesmaid, consider the job a piece of cake. You'll get to run errands for the bride or her mother in the weeks before the wedding, but aside from that, being pretty is their sole responsibility.

THE WEDDING ATTIRE

You can help your wedding party look good by finding dresses, tuxedos and other attire that compliment them. You should look at the color, style, fit and feel of the material as well. You'll also want to keep in mind the theme of your wedding that we talked about in Chapter One. Let's look at how we can save money on wedding attire.

SAVE MONEY BY RENTING

I know you're wondering. Rent a wedding dress? It's not as strange as it might seem. A lot of brides are saying to themselves. Will my daughter really want to wear my wedding dress at her wedding 20-30 years from now? More than likely, NOT! It used to be a grand tradition to get married in white, and spend several hundred dollars to preserve a wedding dress. However, more brides are opting not to wear mom's old wedding dress.

BUY A PROM DRESS

Who can really tell if a prom dress is a prom dress? Prom dresses like wedding dresses are all formal. In addition, prom dresses are usually priced lower than the dresses that are slated for weddings. Don't ask me why, that's just how the designers, retailers do it. Look at the prom dresses before you order dresses for you wedding party. You may be in for a big surprise.

WHAT KIND OF DRESS?

You have your choice of buying the dresses for your wedding or renting. Let's look at what kind of dress would be right for your wedding. You have been thinking about your wedding dress more than likely since you were a little girl. Now is the time to start really looking for one. Before you can decide what kind of dress you want to buy, you have to first decide on what kind of wedding you are going to have.

Remember, the exercise from Chapter One where I asked you to envision your dream wedding. If you completed that exercise then more than likely, you know what you want your dress to look like. But, wait a minute. Let us make sure your idea of a dress matches up with the kind of wedding that you are going to have.

FORMAL/INFORMAL OR NOT

Are you planning on having a formal, informal wedding or something in between the two? Do you want to bare your midriff and make a fashion statement or do you want to take a trip into medieval times. Do not laugh. You may remember from Chapter One that Celtics and Renaissance weddings are among the most common theme weddings. Some people have wonderful wedding celebrations of this kind.

Getting back to you. You may not know what kind of wedding you are going to have just yet. After all, we are just in Chapter Two. By Chapter Six, I am confident you will have it all figured out. You may not know what kind, but you have a good idea of how you want it to look. I believe you will also know the general vicinity of where you want it held. You may even have your guest list sketched in your brain. Whatever is the case, it is a thin line between a formal versus an informal wedding. Let us look at the two.

FORMAL WEDDING

A formal wedding is usually a religious ceremony that takes place at church, cathedral, synagogue, chapel or other worship place. You can have a full reception with assigned, sometime unassigned dinner seating after the wedding. The reception can take place at a variety of places including a country club, museum, hotel, cruise ship, etc. The groom and groomsmen are decked out in tuxedos, suits or other formal wear.

A formal wedding requires the bride to wear either a white, or off-white floor length gown. The train should be cathedral or chapel length with a train about the same size.

SEMI FORMAL WEDDINGS

Semi formal weddings take place at either a chapel, garden, scenic or private home. A semi formal reception can take place at a variety of buffet style or it can be catered under a tent. The bride's gown can be white, off white, or pale pastel. The length of the dress can vary from ankle length to knee length.

The bride can skip wearing a train with a semi formal wedding. You can wear a long or short veil depending on the style of the dress. The groom can dress in a tuxedo or suit. The groomsmen must wear matching clothes. Semi formal wedding skip traditions like a receiving line and announced introductions.

THE INFORMAL WEDDING

An informal wedding is basically any wedding that is not formal or semi-formal. It can happen anytime, anyplace. You set the stage to make the wedding out of the norm. I know a couple that got married in the living room of their parent's home on Thanksgiving Day. I also know another couple that got married with flowered bouquets in their shorts in the Bahamas.

The informal wedding is usually short, sweet and very, very, personal. Sometimes no one else is there but the bride and groom. As you can see, it is very important to decide what kind of wedding you are going to have when you are looking for a gown.

TIME OF YEAR

Winter is not the most popular time of year to get married. Yet, there are some people who do not mind the cold and snow. You will want to make sure you are following the standards based on the time of year. For instance, for a wintertime wedding you will want to wear long sleeves and a higher neckline to help you stay warm.

It used to be a time when wearing strapless gowns in the middle of winter was a fashion no. But, times have changed and now it is okay as long as you are warm. Fur, muffs, boots and gloves are also okay for a bride to wear at a winter wedding.

Fall weddings are beautiful with the falling leaves as a backdrop. A bride may want to choose a gown made out of a medium weight fabric like taffeta or raw silk. Sleeves on the dress are usually kept at three quarter length for a fall wedding. You will want to have a lightweight train. A shawl to help keep the wind off your back.

Spring weddings give the bride to be a chance to show off her style and grace. It is not unusual to see a bride with a pillbox hat on in lieu of a veil. The gown can be made out of a silk tulle, or organza material. A tea length to longer length is also okay depending on what you like. You can also wear cap sleeves or an off the shoulder neckline. It is also okay to pull out the open toed shoes are also okay for a spring wedding.

Summer is the most popular time for nuptials. You have a variety of dresses and fabrics to choose from if you go with this time of year. You can have your pick from short, medium, and ankle length dresses. You can also find styles from halter to backless. The fabric comes in anything from linen to tulle. Thinking about not wearing a veil! Go ahead. Summer is the time of year for a bride to be bold and beautiful. You can wear a flower headpiece to a wide brimmed straw hat. Some brides also opt to go barefoot to sandals.

FOLLOW YOUR STYLE

Let's set aside for a moment the discussion over what size you are and what dresses look best on you. Let's talk about you following your own natural style. You can get married in a wedding dress that reflects the usual essence of you if you know what to look for! Do you follow?

You may be a fancy dresser who loves clothes that flair. If so, then your wedding dress should flair as well. On the other hand, if you are more conservative in your everyday attire, then you'll want a sleeker look for your wedding. You're just following your own sense of style this way

HOW MUCH TO PAY?

This is a big question! I know some people who will bargain show until the find the nicest dress for the most affordable price. Still, there's another school of thought that suggests your wedding dress should be the most expensive dress you'll ever own. In other words, the sky is the limit when you want a wedding dress.

You may want to look at my general wedding budget that I prepared for you in Chapter One. As you can see, I believe the dress, headpiece/veil, lingerie, shoes and accessories fall in the 15% range for your wedding expenses. However, I say feel free to play around with the numbers! If you can cut corners in another way, by all means please do. Designer wedding dresses are the most expensive. They range in price from $1,500 on up! However, you may be able to find a wedding dress on sale for as little as $300.00.

On an average, brides are spending about $800.00 for their dresses. You can also save some money be wearing your mother or grandmothers wedding dresses. Yes, people are still doing that! Bear in mind if you go the "something old" route you will most likely have to pay a little extra for alterations.

A TUX FOR HIM

Okay! That's enough about the female persuasion for right now. Let's talk about attire for him. It's important as well, you know. Let's face it! The man's attire is not as important in a wedding as the woman's attire. Who would dare argue with me on that one? However, tuxes are an important side issue. More and more people are opting to buy tuxes because they figure they'll use them over again during the course of a marriage.

I hope the brides aren't thinking all eyes are going to be on them on D-day! I hope that's not what you're thinking! They guys play an important role in a wedding. They are the first people your guests see. Be sure to pick out a tux that conveys the tone of your wedding.

It's a good thing that tuxedo's are a little more classic today than in yesteryear. Do you remember the ruffled shirts and bow ties from the seventies? Well, they are out now! Nowadays, you can look forward to seeing more conservative shirts, vests, ties and cummerbunds.

RENT OR BUY?

I bet you were wondering how you should handle the question over tuxedos. Should you rent or buys is another good question. Tuxedo's like a wedding and bridesmaids dresses help to set the tone for your overall wedding. Tuxedo's cost anywhere from $300.00 to $500.00 depending on where you buy them.

You will pay about 30 percent of the price of a new tuxedo if you rent a tuxedo. It's also not unusual to be able to buy a good tux in the same place that the bride is buying her gown at. A lot of businesses are making it really convenient for you. If you buy the tux in the same place as the bridesmaids dresses, then it's easier to match up colors.

At the very least, I've noticed some tuxedo shops are open next door to or in the vicinity of dress retailers. I think this will also make it easy for you to match the dress to the tuxedo along with the style and colors. Colored tuxedos are quite popular these days. You can find colored tuxedos in green, lavender, sage, periwinkle and purple. Now, those colors will have everyone talking!

It's my personal preference to go ahead and buy a tux if you're going to go to at least three formal functions during your first year of marriage. You can wear a good tux for years.

TO SUIT OR NOT TO SUIT

A lot of grooms are saying to heck with tuxedos! They are going for the idea of wearing a fine suit on their wedding day. Picking a suit over a tux for a formal wedding is a growing idea. Remember, I talked to you about following your own style. Well, let's suppose that your guy is not a lover of tuxedos. A black on black suit can and will give him the same dashing effect!

ACCESSORIZE HIM

If your man is anything like my man then accessories are not even in his vocabulary! Fix him up on your wedding day and every woman will want him! Make sure the shoes have colored coordinated socks. The shoes that you wear with a tux or suit can lace up or slip on depending on your personal preference. Make sure the shirt has rhinestone, stainless steel, silver or gold cufflinks.

CHAPTER THREE

The Reception

Wedding Savings Trend #3

(You may have not heard about this trend because it's so hot off the market! A member of your family or friends can become temporarily ordained in order to marry you! Hey, don't laugh; you could save in ministerial costs on this one.)

Okay, so having your Uncle Bob marry you may not be your cup of tea. I can't say I'd go for it either. Saving money on your wedding isn't just limited to the wedding itself. The bulk of your savings will come from cutting the costs at your wedding reception. I've had many couples ask me, "Well, do I really have to feed them?" They may have been joking, but my response was a resounding....

YES, YOU'VE GOT TO FEED THEM!

I know some people who have gone so far as to cook the food for the reception and store it in a freezer a week in advance. Still, others have gone to the grocery store to have the reception catered. However, buying from the supermarket is not the only way you can save money on food.

The time of day that you hold your wedding and reception also plays an important role. Take a look at the timetable I've developed. You can save a pretty penny by having your wedding during a time of day when folks are not "as hungry. Take a look at what I mean.

Morning Wedding Ceremony before 11:00am
Continental breakfast or buffet
Midday Wedding 11:00am to 1:00pm
Luncheon buffet

Afternoon Wedding 1:00pm to 4:00pm
Hor d'oeuvres buffet or cake and punch only

Early Evening Wedding 4:00pm to 7:00pm
Dinner buffet

Evening Wedding after 7:00pm
Hors d'oeuvres buffet or cake and punch only

As you can see, the amount of food you'll need to supply at your wedding reception depends on the time of day you hold your reception. Let's now look at the ways you can save in a nutshell! Here's how to do it and do it big! Save as much as 40-60% on your reception costs by following this advice. Here are the **TOP TEN** ways to **SAVE MONEY** on your reception.

SERVE NON ALCOHOLIC DRINKS

You can save a fortune by only serving non-alcoholic drinks at your wedding reception. Some couples are choosing to serve non-alcoholic drinks like sparkling cider or grape juice to their guests. I think this is especially understandable if the couple doesn't drink. Some other couples just serve wine or champagne. In those cases, you can still save money by buying your alcohol in bulk. I'll show you how. Read on.

BUY LIQUOR WHOLESALE

You may decide to go the extra mile and give your guests the option to drink if they want. One way to do this and save money along the way is to buy your liquor direct from a wholesaler. A wholesaler will offer you a discount of up to 20% on bulk purchases of alcohol. A wholesaler will also allow you to return any bottles of liquor that you have not used. By in large this is a great deal.

LIMIT COCKTAIL HOUR

Having an open bar is quite expensive. You can still show your guests a good time and keep the costs down as well. Another way to do this is to limit the amount of time for the cocktail hour. Once the cocktail hour is over, you can then limit drinks to nonalcoholic beverages or wine. I suggest having a host or hostess to pass out the drinks because this helps to prevent waste.

OFF HOUR RECEPTION TIME

We talked a little about this earlier in the book. You can have a breakfast or early afternoon reception and save 30-50% off the reception costs. Breakfast and brunch receptions cost a lot less than dinner receptions do for obvious reasons. Plus, people do not drink as much during the day as they do at night.

SERVE GOOD FOOD NOT EXPENSIVE FOOD

You'll want to go for the lobster and filet mignon meals, however chicken and pasta is just as tasty. Save money by ordering good food, not the most expensive! Also consider having a buffet as opposed to a sit down dinner that costs more.

SERVE EASY HORS D'OEUVRES

Let's face it! You look at some hors d'oeuvres and you just know the cook spent hours in the kitchen making them fancy. I say don't worry about that. Your guests just want something to snack on until din-din arrives. You can have some prepared that aren't expensive requiring hours of preparation time. Also, avoid using hors d'oeuvres that require expensive ingredients.

SERVE THE GUESTS

You'll want to have someone serve your guests rather than have them help themselves for several reasons. For one thing, people have a tendency to take too much food before everyone is served. You want to make sure everyone gets at least one heaping helping!

The worst thing that can happen at your reception is that everyone doesn't get fed. Here is another trick, use small plates. Your guests won't be able to take too much food if it doesn't fit on the plate. They can always come back for more after everyone is served.

EAT AND THROW IT AWAY

Okay, not everyone is going to love this idea! But, I do! You can save lots of money by using paper plates, plastic cups and utensils. You can save up 10-20% over the cost of renting breakable china, glasses and silver.

BE PICKY ICKY WITH YOUR GUEST LIST

You can keep your costs down by keeping your guest list down. You can invite only close friends and business associates. You can do this by asking your guests not to bring dates and children. I know one couple that actually hired a babysitter to watch the kids during the wedding and reception. Now isn't that a great idea. The kids got fed and played while the adults did the same thing!

WAYS TO CREATE A MOOD

MUSIC & ALL THAT JAZZ

You can cut the cost of music with a little ingenuity. How many of us know someone who knows someone who is as good as professional without actually being one? Yes, that's right. I'm suggesting getting an amateur to play and perform at your wedding! No, I'm not crazy. You can save tons of money this way. Take a look at this breakdown.

You can have the friend of a friend or relative of a relative play a musical instrument. It could be a flute, piano or horn. The key to this is to make sure the person is good. Now, you wouldn't want this person to play alone. The cost of your friend's friend will hopefully be nothing. You can have them perform for a short time. Then, you can follow them up with someone who is professional. Someone you do have to pay! The going rates for musicians and singers these days' starts somewhere around $50.00.

Another option is to use the above combination along with some pre-recorded music. I like this option because it gives you a little of both worlds. You can even record you own music using high fidelity recording equipment.

A FLOWER IS JUST A FLOWER, RIGHT? WRONG!

Flowers can make your wedding look and feel more romantic and pretty. It used to be a time when white flowers like lily of the valley or orchids and fern was the style. Thank goodness times have changed! There's nothing wrong with white flowers and fern if that's your style. However, there is a whole new science behind choosing flowers as well as plants that are right for your wedding. Did you know that? First of all you'll want to choose flowers that are in season. Flowers that are in bloom are easier for your florist to get and as a result cheaper as well.

You'll also want to pick fresh flowers that will live longer once they are cut and out of water. Certain flowers hold up better than others. Remember, you have a long day ahead of you that includes picture taking. Your flowers will also have to survive being outdoors in heat or wind. Ask your florist about a hydrator that you can use inside of your bouquet to keep your flowers watered.

If you don't have enough money for live flowers or if your favorite flower is out of season then you may want to think about the unique beauty in silk flowers. The big plus to using silk flowers is that they are less expensive and never die!

You'll want to make a date with the florist to pick out your wedding bouquet. I know too many horror stories where the bride never even saw the flowers before the wedding day. I suggest you find a picture of the flowers that you like in a bridal book. You can show the flowers to your florist and hopefully duplicate the bouquet.

Selecting flowers is not just about what looks pretty to you. Flowers have a meaning. All of them do! Isn't it hard to believe that someone actually took the time to make up the different meanings? It's amazing to me at least. For instance, did you know that a calla lily means, "magnificent beauty" and the fringed gentian means, "I look to heaven?" Add them together and I think you get the picture.

You can create a very special meaning behind the flowers and plants you pick. You can even clue your wedding guests in on the meaning behind your flowers on the back of your wedding program.

Take a look at some of the most popular flowers and what they mean. Put a check by the ones who you like the meaning for and ask your florist to let you see them.

FLOWERS/PLANTS & MEANING

1 **ABUTILON** Meditation
2 **ACACIA** (Rose or white) Elegance, friendship
3 **ACACIA** (yellow) Secret love
4 **ACANTHUS** Artifice, fine arts
5 **ACHILLEA** War
6 **ACONITE** Lustre, misanthropy
7 **ADDER'S-TONGUE** Jealousy
8 **ADONIS** Sad memories
9 **AGRIMONY** Gratitude
10 **ALLSPICE** Compassion
11 **ALMOND** (common) Indiscretion, perfidy
12 **ALOE** grief, misplaced devotion, religious superstition
13 **ASTOREMERIA** Devotion
14 **ALTHEA** Consumed by love
15 **ALYSSYM** (sweet) Excellence
16 **AMARANTH** (coxcomb) Affection, pretension

17 **AMARANTH** (globe) Constant, unchangeable
18 **AMARANTH** Foppery, immortality, pretension
19 **AMARYLLIS** Beautiful, timid, proud
20 **AMBROSIA** Love returned
21 **ANEMONE** Fading hope
22 **ANGELICA** Inspiration, magic
23 **APOCYNUM** Falsehood, figment, I doubt you
24 **APPLE-BLOSSOM** Preference
25 **ARBOR-VITAE** (American) immortality
26 **ARBOR-VITAE** I never change, live for me
27 **ARBUTUS** You only do I love
28 **ASCLEPIAS** Sorrowful remembrance
29 **ASH Prudence** With me you are safe
30 **ASMINE** (night-blooming) Love's vigil
31 **ASPEN** Excess of sensibility, fear
32 **ASTER** (China) Afterthoughts, love of variety
33 **AURICULA** (scarlet) Pride
34 **AURICULA** Painting, wealth is not always
   happiness
35 **AZALEA** Your blush has won me
36 **BACHELOR'S BUTTON** Devotion, hope, love
37 **BALM** Social intercourse, sympathy
38 **BALSAM** Impatience
39 **BAY-LEAF** I change but in death
40 **BABY'S BREATH** Pure of heart
41 **BAYBERRY** Discipline
42 **BEGONIA** Deformity
43 **BELLFLOWER** Constant
44 **BETONY** Surprise
45 **BITTERSWEET** Platonic love
46 **BLUEBELL** Constant
47 **BLUEBOTTLE** Delicacy
48 **BLUETS** Contentment
49 **BORAGE** Talent
50 **BRAMBLE** Holiness
51 **BROOM** Humility

52 **BRYONY** Prosperity
53 **BURDOCK** Importunity
54 **BUTTERCUP** Riches
55 **BUTTERFLY-WEED** Let me go
56 **CACTUS** Grandeur, warmth
57 **CALLA LILY** Magnificent beauty
58 **CALYCANTHUS** Benevolence
59 **CAMELLIA (Red)** Unpretending excellence
60 **CAMELLIA** (White) Perfected loveliness
61 **CHAMOMILE** Energy in adversity
62 **CANDYTUFT** Indifference
63 **CANTERBURY BELLS** Gratitude
64 **CARDINAL-FLOWER** Distinction
65 **CARNATION** Fidelity, love
66 **CARNATION PINK** Woman's love
67 **CATALPA** Beware of the coquette
68 **CATCHFLY** Unchanging friendship
69 **CATTLEYA** Mature charms
70 **CEDAR** I live but for thee
71 **CELANDINE** Joys to come
72 **CENTAURY** Delicacy
73 **CEREUS** (night-blooming) Transient beauty
74 **CHERRY-BLOSSOM** Spiritual beauty
75 **CHESTNUT-BLOSSOM** Do me justice
76 **CHICKWEED** Rendezvous
77 **CHICORY** Frugality
78 **CHRYSANTHEMUM** (Chinese) Loveliness
79 **CHRYSANTHEMUM** (red) I love
80 **CHRYSANTHEMUM** (white) Truth
81 **CINERARIA** Always delighted
82 **CISTUS** Popular
83 **CITRON** Natured beauty
84 **CLEMATIS** Mental Beauty
85 **CLIANTHUS -**Self-seeking, worldliness
86 **CLOTBUR** Rudeness
87 **CLOVER** (four-leafed) Be mine

88 CLOVER (white) Think of me
89 CLOVES Dignity
90 COLTSFOOT Justice shall be done
91 COLUMBINE Folly
92 CONVOLVULUS Uncertainty
93 CORCHORUS Return quickly
94 COREOPSIS Always cheerful
95 CORIANDER Hidden worth
96 CORN-BLOSSOM Riches
97 CORN-COCKLE Peerless and proud
98 CORNEL Success crowned you
99 CORNFLOWER Delicacy, refinement
100COWSLIP You are my divinity
101COXCOMB Foppery
102CRABAPPLE-BLOSSOM Irritability
103CRANBERRY Cure for heartache
104CREEPING CEREUS Modest genius
105CRESS Power, stability
106CROCUS Mirth
107CROWN IMPERIAL Pride of birth
108CURRANT Your frown will destroy me
109CUSCUTA Meanness
110CYCLAMEN Diffidence
111DAFFODIL Unrequited love, regard
112DAHLIA Forever thine
113DAISY (colored) Beauty
114DAISY (Michaelmas) Farewell
115DAISY (white wild) I will think of it
116DAISY Innocence
117DANDELION Love's oracle
118DAPHNE Fame, glory
119DARNEL Vice
120DEW-PLANT Serenade
121DIOSMA Your simple elegance charms me
122DITTANY OF CRETE (white) Passion
123DOCK Patience

124**DODDER OF THYME** Baseness

125**DOGBANE** Falsehood

126**DOGROSE** Pleasure

127**DOGWOOD** Forgetfulness, love undiminished by

128**EGLANTINE** Genius, I wound to heal, poetry, talent

129**ELDER** Compassion, zealousness

130**ENDIVE** Frugality

131**ESCHSCHOLTZIA** Do not refuse me

132**EUPATORIUM** Delay

133**EYEBRIGHT** Cheer up

134**ENNEL** Strength, worthy of praise

135**FERN** Fascination, magic, sincerity

136**FIG Argument**, I keep my secret

137**FILBERT** Reconciliation

138**FIR** Time

139**FLAX** I feel your kindness

140**FLEUR-DE-LIS** Message

141**FLOWER-OF-AN-HOUR** Delicate beauty

142**FLOWERING ALMOND** Hope

143**FORGET-ME-NOT** Constancy, true love

144**FOUR-LEAFED CLOVER** Be mine

145**FOUR-O'CLOCK** Timidity

146**FOXGLOVE** Youth

147**FOXTAIL GRASS** Sporting

148**FUCHSIA** Confiding love

149**FUMITORY** Spleen

150**FURZE** Love for all occasions

151**GARDEN DAISY** Share your sentiments

152**GARDENIA** Refinement

153**GENTIAN** (closed) Sweet be thy dreams

154**GENTIAN** (fringed) I look to heaven

155**GERANIUM** (dark) Melancholy

156**GERANIUM** (fish) Disappointed expectation

157**GERANIUM** (horseshoe) Stupidity

158**GERANIUM** (Ivy) Favour

159GERANIUM (lemon) Unexpected meeting
160GERANIUM (nutmeg) Expected meeting
161GERANIUM (oak) True friendship
162GERANIUM (pencilled) Ingenuity
163GERANIUM (rose) Preference
164GERANIUM (scarlet) Comforting
165GERANIUM (silver leafed) Recall
166GERANIUM (wild) Steadfast piety
167GERANIUM Gentility, peaceful mind
168GILLYFLOWER Bonds of affection
169GLADIOLUS Ready-armed
170**GOLDENROD** Encouragement
171GOOSEBERRY Anticipation
172GRANDIFLORA High-souled
173GRAPE (wild) Charity, mirth
174**GRASS** Submission
175**HANDFLOWER** Warning
176**HAREBELL** Submission
177HARLEQUIN Laugh at trouble
178HAWKWEED Quick-sighted
179**HAWTHORN** Hope
180**HAZEL** Reconciliation
181**HEARTSEASE** Think of me
182**HEATH** Solitude
183**HELENIUM,** Tears
184HELIOTROPE Eagerness, intoxicated with joy
185HELLEBORE Devotion
186HEMLOCK You will cause my death
187**HEMP** Fate
188**HIBISCUS** Delicate beauty
189HOLLY Domestic happiness
190HOLLYHOCK Ambition
191HONEY-FLOWER Love sweet and secret
192HONEYSUCKLE (coral) Fidelity,
193**HONEYSUCKLE** Bonds of love
194**HOP** Injustice

195**HORNBEAM** Ornament
196**HORSE-CHESTNUT** Luxury
197**HOUSELEEK** Vivacity
198**HOUSTONIA** Contentment
199**HYACINTH** (purple) Jealousy
200**HYACINTH** (white) Modest loveliness
201**HYACINTH** Constancy
202**HYDRANGEA** Boaster
203**HYSSOP** Cleanliness
204**ICE-PLANT** Your looks freeze me
205**IRIS (German)** Aflame
206**IRIS Message** Eloquence
207**IVY Fidelity** Friendship, marriage, wedded love
208**JACOB'S-LADDER** Come down
209**JASMINE** (cape) I am too happy
210**JASMINE** (Carolina) Separation
211**JASMINE** (Indian) I attach myself to you
212**JASMINE** (Spanish) Sensuality
213**JASMINE** (white) Amiability
214**JASMINE** (yellow) Grace and elegance
215**JASMINE** I am too happy
216**JONQUIL** I desire a return of your affection
217**JUDAS-TREE** Unbelief
218**KINGCUP** Riches
219**LABURNUM** Forsaken, pensive beauty
220**LADY'S SLIPPER** Capricious beauty
221**LADY'S SMOCK** Ardor
222**LADY'S THIMBLE** Submission
223**LADY'S-TRESSES** Bewitching grace
224**LANTANA** I am unyielding
225**LARCH** Boldness
226**LAUREL** (ground) Perseverance
227**LAUREL** (mountain) Ambition
228**LAUREL** Perfidy
229**LAURESTINE** I die if neglected
230**LAVENDER** Acknowledgment

231**LEMON** Discretion
232**LETTUCE** Cold-hearted
233LICHEN Solitude
234**LILAC** (purple) First love
235**LILAC** (white) Youthful innocence
236**LILY** (water) Purity of heart
237LILY (calla) Maiden modesty, beauty
238LILY (day) Coquetry
239LILY (frog) Disgust
240**LILY** (tiger) I dare you to love me
241LILY (white) Purity and sweetness
242LILY (yellow) Flirtation
243**LILY-OF-THE-VALLEY** Return of happiness
244**LINDEN** Conjugal love
245**LIVE-OAK** Liberty
246**LIVERWORT** Confidence
247LOBELIA Arrogance
248LOCUST Affection beyond the grave
249**LONDON-PRIDE** Frivolity
250LOTUS Estranged love
251**LOVE-IN-A-MIST** Perplexity
252**LOVE-LIES** Hopeless but not heartless
253**LUCERNE** Life
254**LUPINE** (rose) Fanciful
255**LUPINE** (white) Always happy
256LUPINE Voraciousness
257**MAGNOLIA -** Nobility
258**MISTLETOE -** Kiss me
259**MOSS -** Charity
260**MYRTLE –** Love
261NARCISSUS Stay as Sweet as You Are
262NASTURTIUM - Conquest, Victory in Battle
263**OLEANDER -** Caution
264**ORANGE BLOSSOM -** Eternal Love
265**ORCHID -** Beautiful Lady
266**ORCHID (CATTLEYA)** - Mature Charm

267PALM LEAVES - *Victory and Success*
268PEONY - Happy Life and Marriage
269PETUNIA - Your Presence Sooths Me
270PINE – Hope
271POPPY (GENERAL) - Imagination
272POPPY (RED) - Pleasure
273POPPY (WHITE) – Consolation
274POPPY (YELLOW) - Wealth, Success
275PRIMROSE - I Can't Live Without You
276PRIMROSE (EVENING) - Inconstancy
277ROSE (BRIDAL) - Happy Love
278ROSE (DARK CRIMSON) - Mourning
279ROSE (HIBISCUS) - Delicate Beauty
280ROSE (LEAF) - You May Hope
281ROSE (PINK) - Perfect Happiness
282ROSE (RED) - Love, I Love You
283ROSE (TEA) - I'll Remember Always
284ROSE (THORNLESS) - Love at First Sight
285ROSE (WHITE) - Innocence and Purity
286ROSE (WHITE AND RED MIXED) – Unity
287ROSE (WHITE-DRIED) - Death
288ROSE (YELLOW) - Try to Care
289ROSEBUD - A Heart Innocent of Love
290ROSEBUD (RED) - Pure and Lovely
291ROSEBUD (WHITE) - Girlhood
292ROSEBUD (MOSS) - Confessions of Love
293ROSES (Bouquet of Mature Blooms) - Gratitude
294ROSES (Single Full Bloom) - I Love You
295SMILAX - Loveliness
296SNAPDRAGON - Gracious Lady
297SPIDER FLOWER - Elope with Me
298STEPHANOTIS - Happiness in Marriage
299STOCK - You'll Always Be Beautiful to Me
300SWEETPEA - Thank You for a Lovely Time
301TULIP (GENERAL) - Perfect Lover
302TULIP (RED) - Believe Me

303TULIP (VARIEGATED) - Beautiful Eyes
304TULIP (YELLOW) - There's Sunshine in Your
    Smile
305VIOLET - Modesty
306VIOLET (BLUE) - I'll Always Be True
307VIOLET (WHITE) - Let's Take a Chance
308ZINNIA (MAGENTA) - Lasting affection
309ZINNIA (MIXED) – Thinking of an absent friend
310ZINNIA (SCARLET) - Constancy
311ZINNIA (WHITE) - Goodness
312ZINNIA (YELLOW) - Daily Remembrance

Can you find a flower, maybe two or three out of all of these that you'd like to have in your wedding because of the meaning?   There is a rhyme and reason behind picking a flower type. But, there is also a reason why you should be choosy over the size of your bouquet. It's not like the flowers are being delivered to you so you want the biggest and the biggest! You want your flowers to add to the beauty of your dress. You don't you're your flowers to overwhelm you. Your flowers should accentuate your waistline when you're holding them.

Now, I'd like to share with you a few tips to getting the most out of your wedding flowers. You can give away the corsages and boutonnieres to family, friends and other wedding guests. You can even give the flowers to your clergy, musician or disc jockey. Everyone loves flowers! I was recently at a wedding where the flower centerpiece was given away to one lucky person sitting at the reception table. I won one much to my surprise! I never win anything by the way.

Finally, when choosing a flower it's not just the looks and meaning that are important. They should smell good as well. Gardenias, tuberoses, and peonies are some of the most fragrant smelling flowers.

CHAPTER FOUR

Video & Photography

Wedding Savings Trend #4

(More and more couples are using black and white film for their wedding pictures. If that trend doesn't suit your fancy, you can always put a one-time use color camera on the reception tables and let your guests help to be the photographer.)

Let's look at some other options if temporarily ordaining your brother to marry you doesn't sound like your cup of tea! You can save you hundreds of dollars off of your videographer/photographers rates while preserving the memories. Think about the last wedding that you attended. What was special about it?

Chances are if you're having a tough time remembering the highlights, then the couple is as well. That's why photographs and video are so important. You may remember that the cake tasted good. You may remember that Uncle Bob made a drunken fool of himself. You made a hit out of Barbara Streisand's "Memories." Nothing! And, I mean nothing plays as well and for so long as video and photograph.

SKIMPING WITHOUT MISSING A SHOT

Most couples decide to have a videographer and a photographer at the wedding. It can be very expensive hiring both. The professional rates begin as little as $100.00 an hour. It's well worth it if you ask me. There's nothing like a person with an "eye" that knows what to look for in pictures.

Let's go over the pros and cons of still and video shots. I know you're interested in saving a buck! However, I know you're much more concerned about saving your memories. Let's see how we can accomplish both goals.

VIDEOTAPE

The popularity of having a videotape of your wedding has grown throughout the years. One of the best things about video is that you can see the product right away. A skilled videographer actually shoots the video and edits the shot as he goes along. Professional shooters call this video "raw" footage. You can get a copy of the video right after your wedding. However, you can also have the footage cut into a nice video packaged piece. A wedding video package can range starting at up to $2,500. The price includes the cost of the videographer, tape and 2-3 copies.

PHOTOGRAPHS

A videotape may give you immediate access to your wedding memories, however still photos are good to have as well. The trends show that couples are sticking with this more traditional way to preserve memories. In fact, they are paying more and more for it.

An average wedding package includes 4 8X10's, forty 4X5's and a leather album. Wedding photographer can cost you as much as $1,500 per event. You can get other photographs for an additional price. A good photographer and videograper will help you to capture the moment without being intrusive to you and guests.

There's an easy way to help make sure that you receive all the pictures that you want on your wedding day. I'm going to give you what is called a shot sheet to pass on to your photographer. This sheet will ensure that you get all the right still and video pictures.

40 POINT- PHOTOGRAPHY/VIDEO SHOT SHEET

Before Wedding

Morning sunrise
Bride gets ready the morning of wedding with bridesmaids
Nervous groom waits

Ceremony

1 Bride with bouquet
2 Bride and father walking up the aisle
3 Kneeling in prayer
4 The lighting of the unity candle
5 The exchange of vows
6 The first kiss
7 The couple walking down the aisle.

After Ceremony

1 Bride and groom with parents
2 Bride with her mother
3 Groom with his mother
4 Bride with her father
5 Groom with his father
6 Bride with her grandparents

7   Groom with his grandparents
8   Bride with the children in wedding
9   Groom with the children in wedding
10 Bride with bridesmaids
11 Groom with groomsmen
12 Bride with groomsmen
13 Groom with bridesmaids
14 Bride with maid or matron of honor
15 Groom with best man
16 The entire wedding party

Reception

1   Food
2   Special decorations
3   Couple arrives at reception
4   The couples first dance
5   The bride dancing with her father
6   The groom dancing with his mother
7   The best man's toast
8   The cake cutting
9   The couple feeds each other
10 Rings
11 Brides bouquet toss
12 Bride and whoever caught the bouquet
13 Groom takes off the brides garter
14 Groom's garter toss
15 Groom and whoever caught the bouquet
16 Bride and groom leaving reception
17 Bride and grooms drive away

CHAPTER FIVE

The Honeymooners

Wedding Savings Trend #5
*(Have you heard about honeymoon registries? That's
right. Honeymoon registries actually allow gift givers to
help pay for your honeymoon through their contributions.
Gift givers can also pay for certain activities for you in
advance while you're on your honeymoon. What a great
idea, huh? And to think, it saves you some money as well.
Let's see what would you rather have a 3rd toaster or a
scuba diving lesson?)*

Let's spend the money now that I've saved you a
boatload of money on your wedding and reception! Just
joking. You can continue the saving spree well into the
first year of you marriage if you like. Or, you can do what
I'd do. HAVE A GREAT TIME! Nevertheless, I'm going
to continue in the great spirit of this book by telling you
how to save more money on the honeymoon. Let's go.

I'm excited that we've reached this point in our
book. Remember at the very beginning I told you that we'd
save enough money to spend it all on the honeymoon?
Well, we're at the point now where we can start talking
about planning the honeymoon. I want to continue to give
you some valuable advice on spending for the honeymoon.
Here we go.

THE EARLY BIRD

If you follow the wedding planning calendar that
I've outlined in Chapter 6, then you know that you should

start planning the honeymoon early. I suggest working with a travel agent who can help you figure out the best trip fro you. They also can give you discounts based on their high sales volume. Travel agents are also experts on the trends in the business so they can help you find the best deal.

You should look for an agent that specializes in cruises if you want to go on that type of honeymoon. If you don't want to use a travel agent, then you can also check out the tourist office in the place where you want to honeymoon to get free hotel and activities information. Let's take a look at my **14-STEP GUIDE TO FINDING RED LIGHT HONEYMOON SPECIALS.**

BOOK THE TRIP ONLINE

It doesn't matter if you're booking a trip several months ahead of time or last minute in a lot of cases if you book your trip online. You can find some really great deals this way. There are several websites that you can find that offer these deals. Check out our resource guide at the end of the book for more information.

SHOP FOR THE HONEYMOON, BEFORE IT

You may hear people talking about waiting to buy once you get to your honeymoon destination. I can tell you that prices are always inflated for tourists. You don't want to wait to shop. Start looking around for bargains before the big day. You'll be glad you did. You can usually find good deals on film, batteries, toiletries, etc. ahead of time.

SHOP FOR THE HONEYMOON, DURING IT

I just told you how to save money before the honeymoon. Now, let's talk a little bit about how you can save money during the honeymoon. I suggest that you visit many stores during your day out on the town. Simply shop around before settling on any one item.

You'll find prices vary from store to store. In a lot of cases, the stores carry the same merchandise because there are certain items that are unique to that part of the world. Shop around during your honeymoon for the best prices and don't be afraid to try to barter the sales people down.

PLAN AN OFF SEASON HONEYMOON

Who wants to go to Jamaica in the height of summer? Who wants to go to Europe in the fall? Who in the world would ever dream of going to Australia in the winter? You do, that's who especially if it means saving hundreds of dollars! Here's something important to note. Off-season doesn't necessarily mean bad weather. A lot of people assume it does.

Off-season simply means that fewer people are traveling to these destinations for a variety of reasons. It could have something to do with the end of summer break and the beginning of the school season. It's really hard to tell in some cases. However, the important thing to note for you is that there are advantages to planning an off-season honeymoon.

One of the biggest advantages is you'll get cheaper prices on hotel and airfare. That's because there are fewer people traveling during off-season. You'll also get better service from cab drivers, tour guides, hotel and restaurant employees, etc. They'll just be glad to see you around because the crowds won't be around.

CHEAPER DESTINATIONS

Going to a cheaper destination does not mean that you won't have a good time. Places like Mexico and Canada are more affordable based on their low currency rates. Other places like the Bahamas and Jamaica are so frequently traveled that it has helped to bring down the rates. Choosing a cheaper destination could be an economically healthy alternative for you.

CLOSE TO HOME

There are several advantages to staying close to home for your honeymoon. You save time, money and a lot of hassle that comes from traveling if you drive. I know a lot of couples that were able to upgrade to better accommodations because they decided to drive to a local resort.

EAT SMART

Here's a tip that very few penny pinchers ever think about. At least, they're always in shock when I bring it up! There's always that "must eat at" restaurant in every travel destination. It's usually a five star restaurant with great food, service and high prices. Well, try eating at this place for lunch instead of dinner.

Lunch prices are usually more affordable. Plus, if you don't like the food, then you won't be stuck with a high tab. If you like the food, then say what the heck!

Splurge! Go back for dinner, but let it be your choice to spend the big bucks, not theirs. Also, don't forget to ask about Happy Hours. It's another great way to have fun and save money.

USE ALTERNATIVE TRAVEL PLANS

Instead of taking a plane, why not ride the rails? The train is a cost effective alternative to flying. If you're not honeymooning too far from home, then taking a scenic bus ride may be nice as well. You can plan to make several stops along the way to make the trip more exciting if you're going a long distance.

FREQUENT FLYIER MILES

I know many couples that have gotten to their honeymoon destination this way. While you're at it, check into other membership rewards that might come along with hotel and car rentals as well.

AIR PASS IT TO FAR AWAY

This option is available on airlines that service some of the foreign destinations like Europe and South America. These tickets let you travel to different countries as long as they are within a certain region. Trying to get a good deal on an air pass is well worth the effort.

Some hotels and airlines are offering great deals to people who make their reservations online. Some sites like priceline.com actually lets you pick your own price as long as your travel day, time and place to stay are flexible.

ALL INCLUSIVES AN ALL AROUND GOOD DEAL

All-inclusive are a great deal for people who want to pay for it and enjoy their honeymoon worry free. Most all-inclusive package deals cover the room, meals, drinks and entertainment. Did I forget to mention, tours, taxis, taxes and tips as well? Yes, it's true. Be sure to find out what an all-inclusive covers because it varies from one company to another.

CONDO OR VILLA IT!

If you pick this cost saving measure, you can save a pretty penny on meals. Oh, so you don't want to cook on your honeymoon. I can understand that. The upside to a condo or villa is the romantic meals with candlelight and low music. Get the picture now? Choosing this option is NOT all work!

HOTELS OFFER GREAT DEALS

They don't advertise this deal so you'll have to call around to check on prices. You can have your reception at some hotels and they'll throw in a honeymoon suite free. You can also get discounts on rooms for your guests.

HONEYMOON BUDGET SWEET 'N SIMPLE

Let's turn from saving money on your honeymoon costs to tracking and planning your exact honeymoon costs. You may be thinking okay; I know what my budget is. It's $1,000. End of subject. Well, it's not so easy. In order for you to meet your $1,000 budget, you have to have everything itemized. This section will help you to do that.

Let's break it down with my **EASY TO TABULATE HONEYMOON BUDGET TABLE.**

MAJOR TRANSPORTATION

AIR, RAIL, or SHIP)_____

RENTAL CAR_____

GAS_____

TAXI & TIPS_____

TOTAL TRANSPORATION_____

ACCOMMODATIONS
Hotel_____

Resort_____

SERVICES_____
(Spa, Dry Cleaners)

TOTAL ACCOMMODATIONS___
_____

FOOD
Breakfast (daily x number of days)
Lunch   (daily x number of days)

Dinner   (daily x number of days)
Snacks   (daily x number of days)

**TOTAL
MEALS**_____
____

ENTERTAINMENT
Theater & Concerts_____

Nightclubs_____

Sightseeing_____

Athletic Rental_____

**TOTAL
ENTERTAINMENT**_____
___

GIFTS & SOUVENUERS_____

**TOTAL
BUDGET**_____
(Add totals)

CHAPTER SIX

The Timeline

Wedding Savings Trend #6
(I saved the best for last! This is the savings trend of all savings trends! Get married over Thanksgiving Dinner. Or, Christmas. The Fourth of July even! More and more couples are opting this as a way to kill two birds with one stone. You don't have to worry about paying for a reception hall if you don't want to. You don't have to worry about paying for extra food if you don't want to! I believe this is the ULTIMATE wedding savings trend.)

We're near the end now and it's a bitter-sweet feeling for me. I've enjoyed passing on these helpful tips to you. Let's see. In Chapter One, we looked at the things you should do as soon as you know you're going to get married. In Chapter Two we looked at what your wedding party, what kind of attire you should wear and how you should depend on your own sense of style.

Chapter Three, we went over the top ten ways to save money on your reception. Plus, we found out how to skimp without missing a shot using our 40-point picture shot sheet in Chapter Four. In Chapter Five we learned how to find the honeymoon red light specials. Now, in Chapter Six, we're ready for our Four Month Wedding Countdown Calendar. Follow my time suggestions on this calendar and you will have a less stressed time! Here's what the calendar looks like:

THE WEDDING COUNTDOWN CALENDAR

FOUR MONTHS and counting

1 Finish making plans for the reception
2 Finish the guest list
3 Order invitations and thank you notes
4 Order wedding cake
5 Select a photography/videography plan
6 Select a floral and music
7 Select the food menu

THREE MONTHS and counting

1 Write out the wedding ceremony
2 Write out your own vows if you want
3 Reserve tuxedos
4 Make a doctors appointment to get blood tests
5 Start addressing invitations

TWO MONTHS and counting

1 Mail invitations
2 Write thank you notes for any gifts you've received so far
3 Make a shot list for the videographer and photographer
4 Start practicing hairstyles
5 Pick the music

ONE MONTH and counting

1 Get a marriage license
2 Place a wedding announcement in the newspaper
3 Address wedding announcements for people who aren't coming to wedding

4   Write thank you notes for gifts you've already received
5   Set a date for the final fitting of the wedding dress
6   Loosen your wedding shoes up by wearing them around the house
7   Buy luggage if you don't already have
8   Plan rehearsal dinner

THREE WEEKS and counting

1   Double check to make sure everyone is measured for tuxedo
2   Finalize rehearsal and rehearsal dinner plans
3   Choose transportation for wedding party on wedding day

TWO WEEKS and counting

1   Confirm the reception guest list with caterer
2   Give photographer and videographer a shot list
3   Pack for the honeymoon
4   Determine wedding ceremony, reception and rehearsal dinner seating

ONE WEEK and counting

1   Confirm the arrangements
2   Florist, caterer, photographer
3   Honeymoon, bridal suite, airline tickets, travelers checks.
4   Final fitting of wedding gown
5   Bridesmaids luncheon
6   Confirm rehearsal plans

Planning a wedding is that simple! I hope you have had as much of a good time reading this book as I have had writing it. As you can see, you don't have to be rich to plan an elegant wedding. You don't have to be the most organized person, either. Just follow my guidelines and you'll be living a life in love forever after, forever. Here's to you and a happy future together!

WEDDING RESOURCES:

BRIDAL CONSULTANTS

Association of Bridal Consultants
(860) 355-0464
www.bridalassn.com

BRIDAL REGISTRIES

Macy's Wedding Channel
www.MACYS.WEDDINGCHANNEL.COM

Neiman Marcus
www.neimanmarcus.com

Target
(800) 888-9333
www.target.com

The Home Depot
www.homedepot.com

WEDDING INVITATIONS

www.weddingbells.com

WEDDING VIDEOGRAPHY

Wedding and Event Videographers Association
International (WEVA) 800 501-WEVA
www.weva.com

WEDDING WEBSITES

www.brides.com

www.bridesave.com

www.theknot.com

www.todaysbride.com

www.ultimatewedding.com

www.weddingchannel.com

EXPERTS ON RELIGIOUS REQUIREMENTS

Beth Din of America (Jewish)
www.bethdin.org

Church of Jesus Christ of Latter Day Saints
(Mormon)
http://www.lds.org

Evangelical Lutheran Church in America
www.elca.org

General Council Assemblies of God
www.ag.org

Greek Orthodox Archdiocese of America
www.goarch.org

Presbyterian Center, News Services Office
www.pcusa.org

Quaker Information Center
www.afsc.org/qic.htm

Union of American Hebrew Reform
(Jewish/Reform)
www.uahc.org

Unitarian Universalist Association
www.uua.org

BUSINESS CHECK

Council of Better Business Bureaus
www.bbbonline.org

Consumer Information Center
www.pueblo.gsa.gov

FLOWERS

Teleflora (Free brochures)
www.teleflora.com

VIDEOGRAPHER AND PHOTOGRAPHY

Professional Photographers of America, Inc.
www.ppa.com

Wedding and Portrait Photographers International

www.wppi-online.com

WEDDING MUSIC

American Federation of Musicians
www.afm.org

American Society of Composers, Authors and
Publishers
www.ascap.com

WEDDING REGISTRY'S

Crate & Barrel
www.crateandbarrel.com

Honeymoon Registry Websites
www.thehoneymoon.com

Target Stores
www.target.com

Tiffany & Co.
www.tiffany.com

Williams-Sonoma
www.williams-sonoma.com

WEDDING TRAVEL

www.travel.state.gov

Amtrak
www.amtrak.com

Consumer Reports Travel Letter
www.consumerreports/org/services/travel.html

Cruise Lines International Association
www.cruising.org

Travel Health Services
www.travelhealth.net